By Bill Plympton

NANTIER ◦ BEALL ◦ MINOUSTCHINE
Publishing inc.
new york

Bill Plympton

Born in Portland, Oregon on April 30, 1946, Bill credits Oregon's rainy climate for nurturing his drawing skills and imagination. In 1964 he graduated from Oregon City High School and went on to Portland State University, where he edited the yearbook and was a member of the film society. It was for this film society that he first attempted animation, making a yearbook promo that was accidentally shot upside-down, rendering it totally useless.

In 1968, he moved to New York City and served a long tenure as an illustrator and cartoonist, doing illustrations for The New York Times, Vogue, House Beautiful, The Village Voice, Screw, and Vanity Fair. In 1975, in The Soho Weekly News, he began "Plympton", a political cartoon strip. By 1981, it was syndicated in over twenty papers by Universal Press.

Collections of his drawings include "Tube Strips", 1975, Smyrna Press, "Medium Rare", 1976, Holt, Reinhart and Winston, and "Polls Apart", 1984, from Dolphin Books.

Immediately following the completion of "Boomtown", his first animated short in 1983, he began his own animated film, "Your Face" which garnered a 1988 Oscar nomination for best animation.

His work started appearing with more and more frequency on MTV and showing in the increasingly popular touring animation festivals. After a string of highly successful short films ("One of Those Days", "How to Kiss", "25 Ways to Quit Smoking", and "Plymptoons"), he began "The Tune", the first full-length animated feature drawn by one person, released nationwide in 1992.

In addition to completing another animated feature, titled "I Married a Strange Person", Plympton has created a theatrical compilation of his short films, "Mondo Plympton", and has been featured in a documentary called "Twisted Toons" about the making of the film "The Tune". In addition to his very successful video "Plymptoons", he has released a comic book featuring the best of his cartoons from men's magazines, called "The Sleazy Cartoons of Bill Plympton" and another collection of his one-panel cartoons called "We Eat Tonight".

He also recently enjoyed a brief stellar career as model for GAP for their khaki shorts.

Bill is working on making an animated feature film of "Mutant Aliens" which should be completed in the fall of 2000. His short films can be seen at www.atom-films.com and more information on Bill is available at www.awn.com/plympton/.

NOTE FROM BILL PLYMPTON

I'm very excited to present this graphic novel from my new feature film "Mutant Aliens".

In 1996, I put together a crude book out of the storyboard drawings from "I Married a Strange Person" and it became very successful.

So, during the storyboard process of my new animated feature "Mutant Aliens", I decided to draw the sketches with much more detail and personality than usual. This helped me in the animation stage to resolve a lot of the visual details.

Just be aware that, as part of my creative process, great ideas will often occur to me in the middle of animating a scene, sou you will observe a few differences between this book and the finished film.

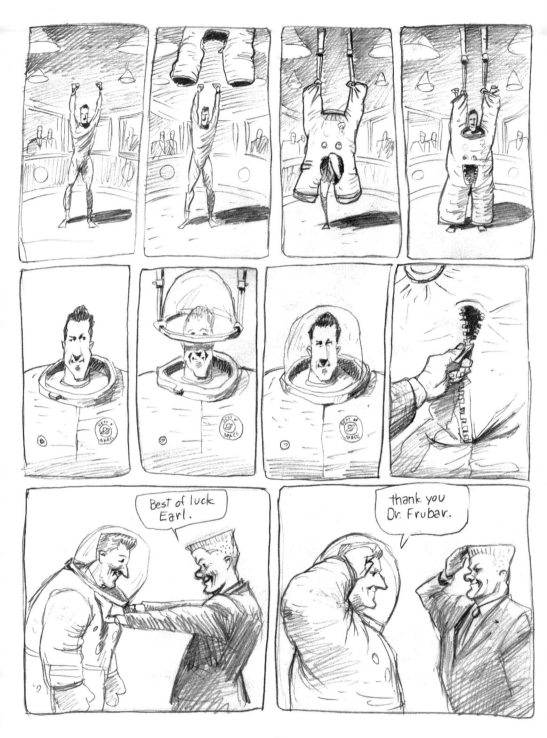

11

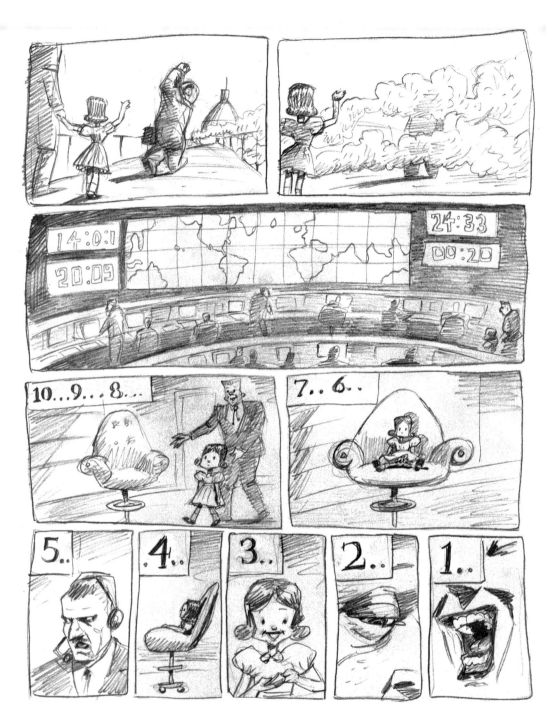

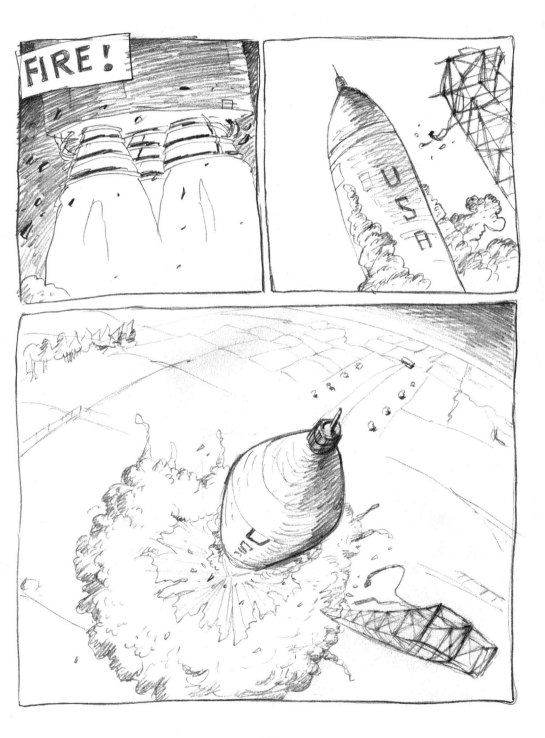

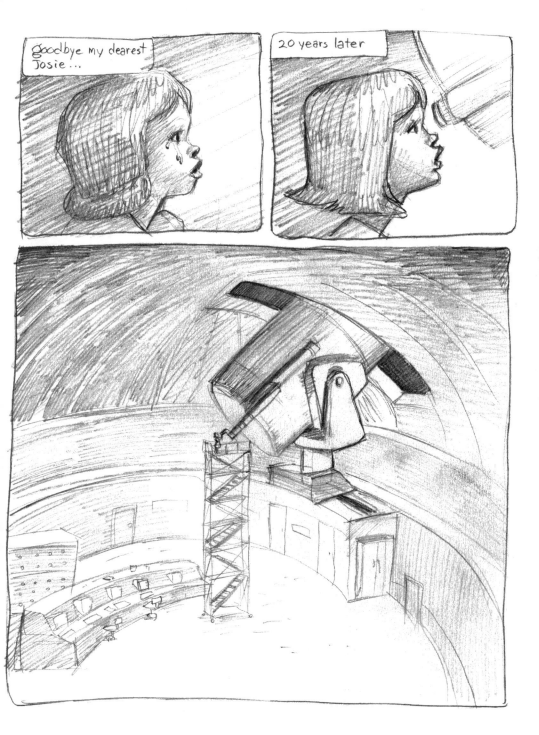

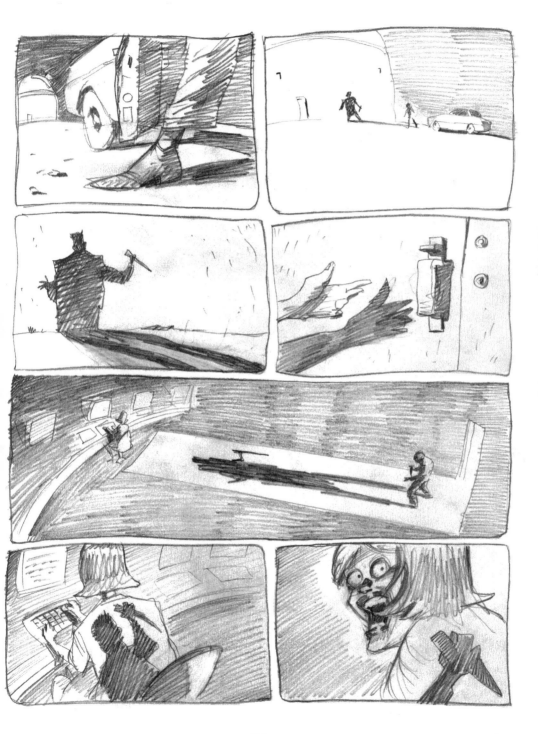

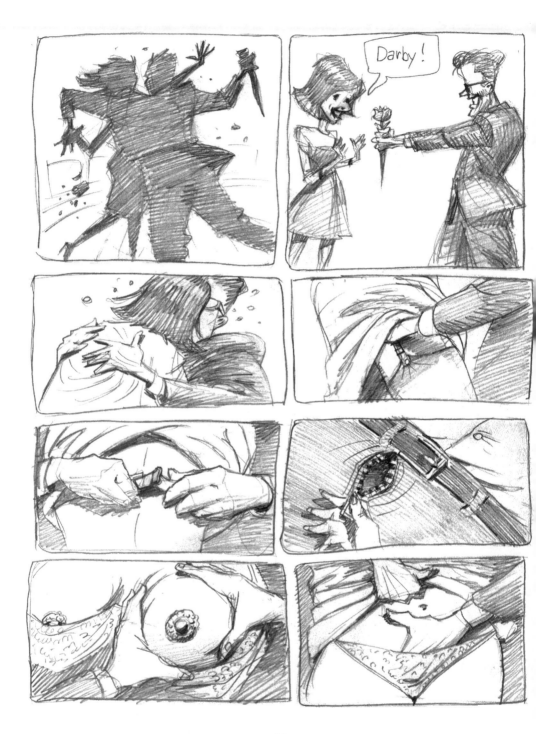

Hello, Dept of space - this is Josie here at the observ..
Josie, why don't you get married and stop bothering us!
Trust me! check coordinates 63428-711025!
o.k. Josie
What a great view!
Dr. F they're on their way down.

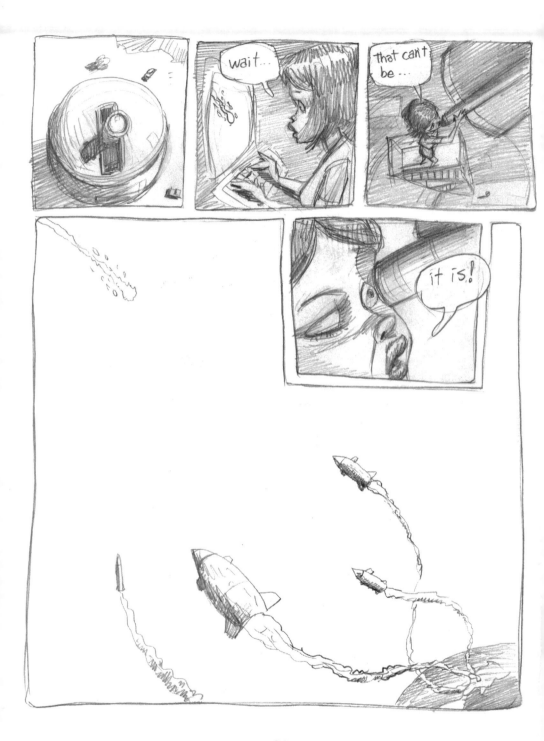

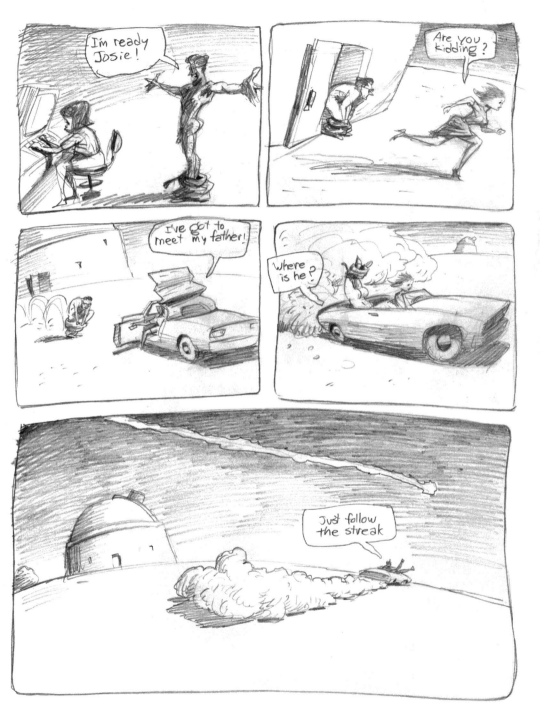

38

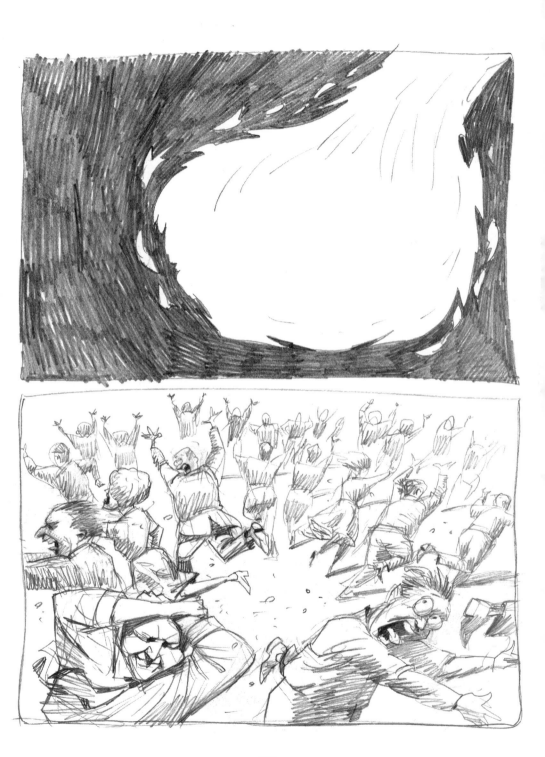

43

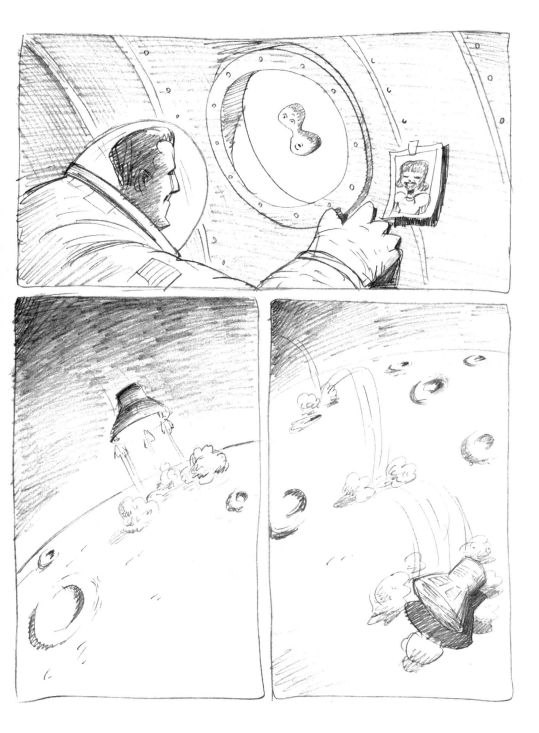

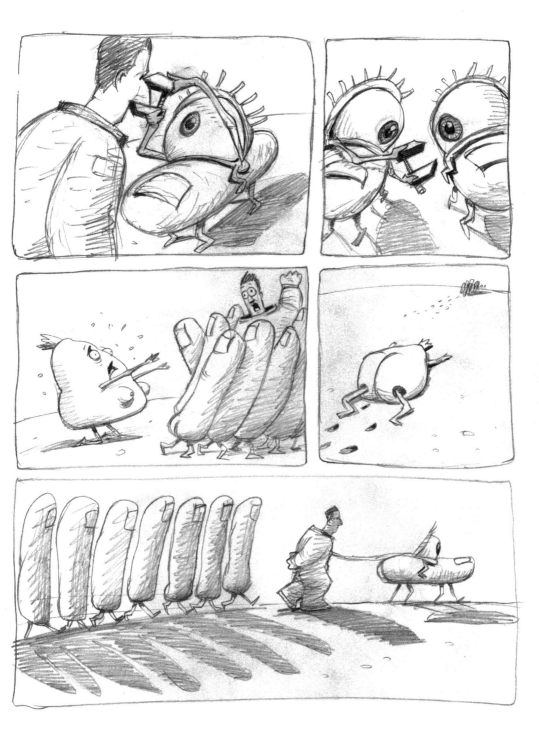

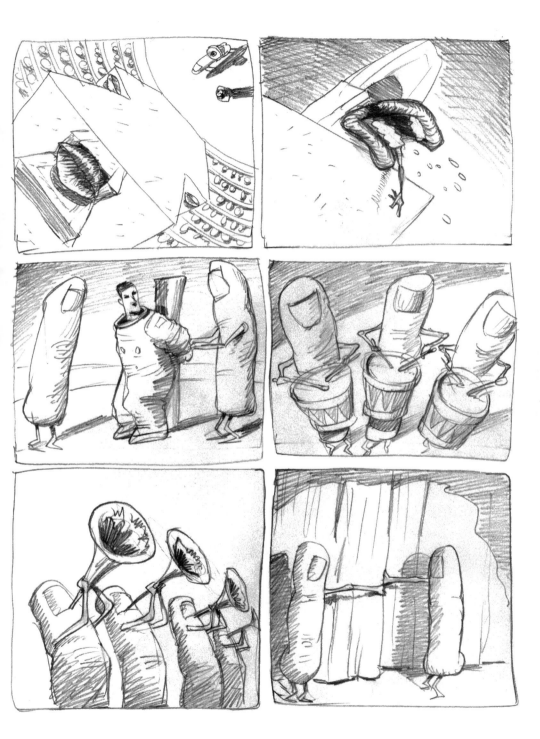

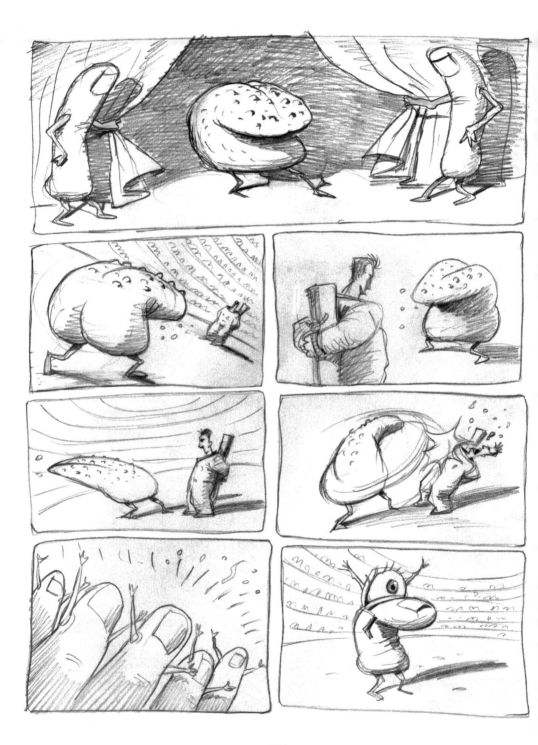

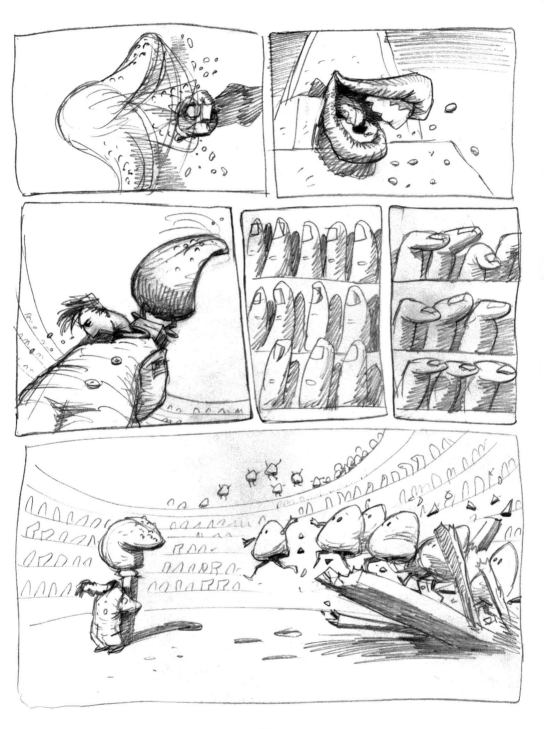

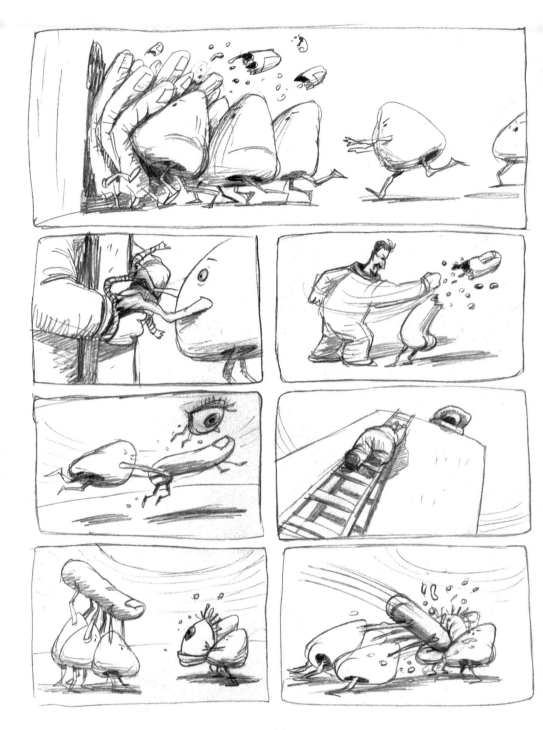

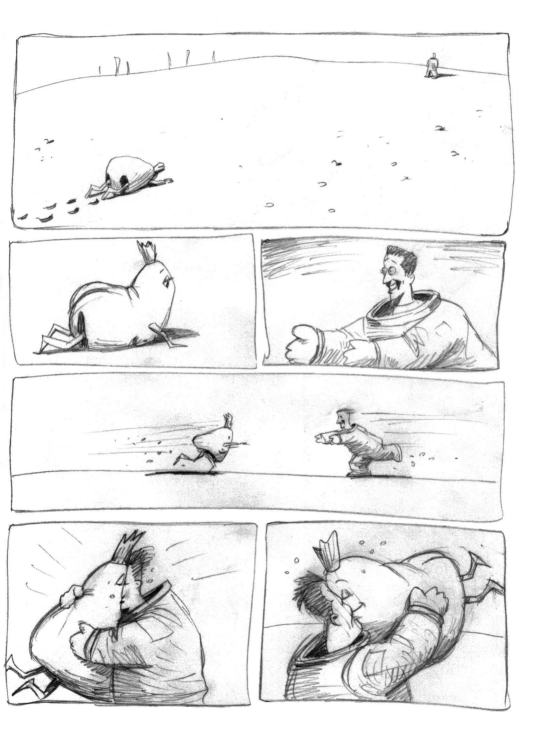

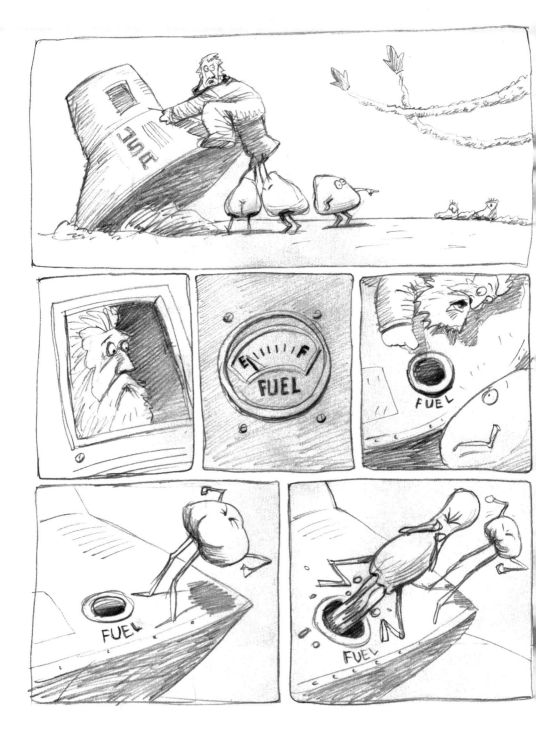

BWAAAH! HAH! HAH!

I'm going to meet Dr. F at the White House next week.

76

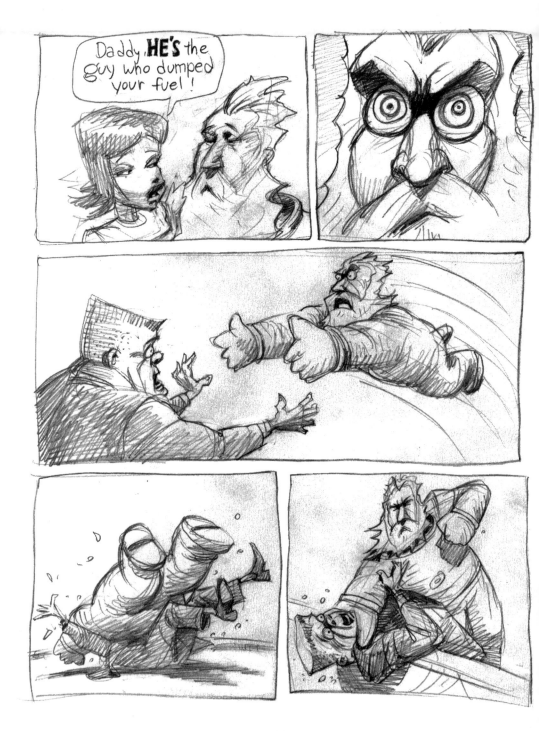

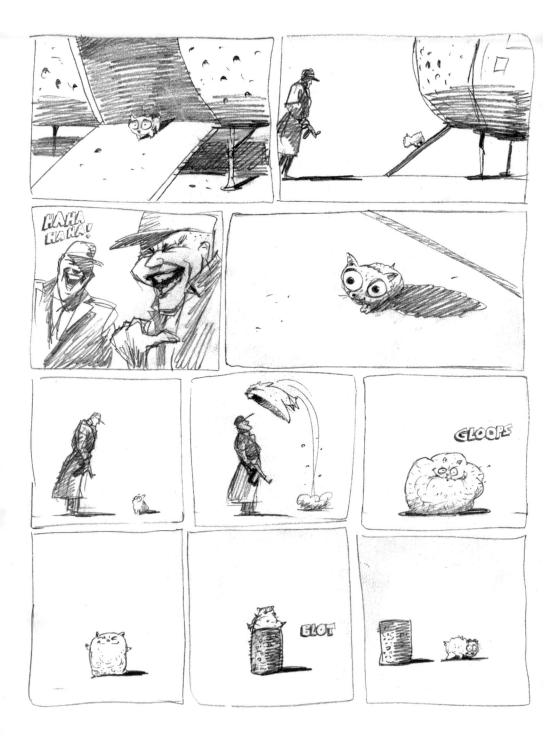

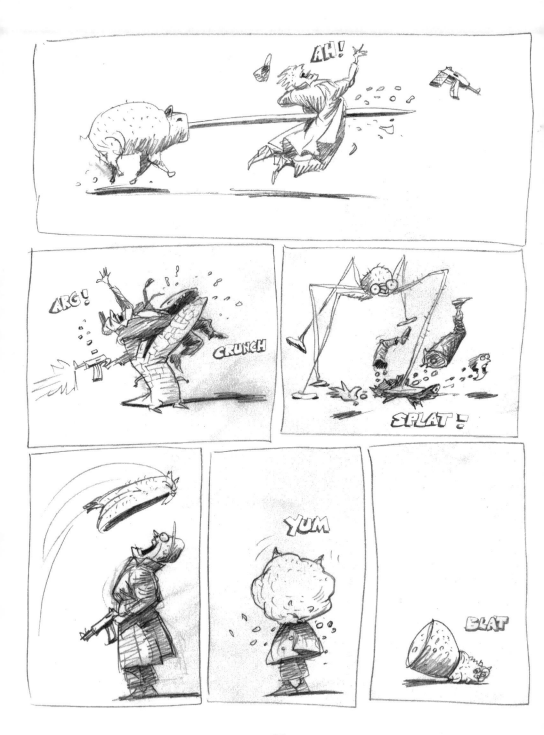

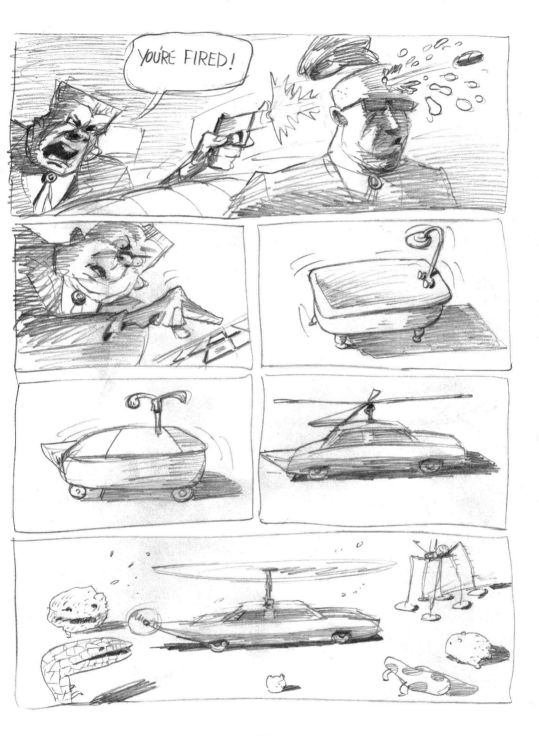

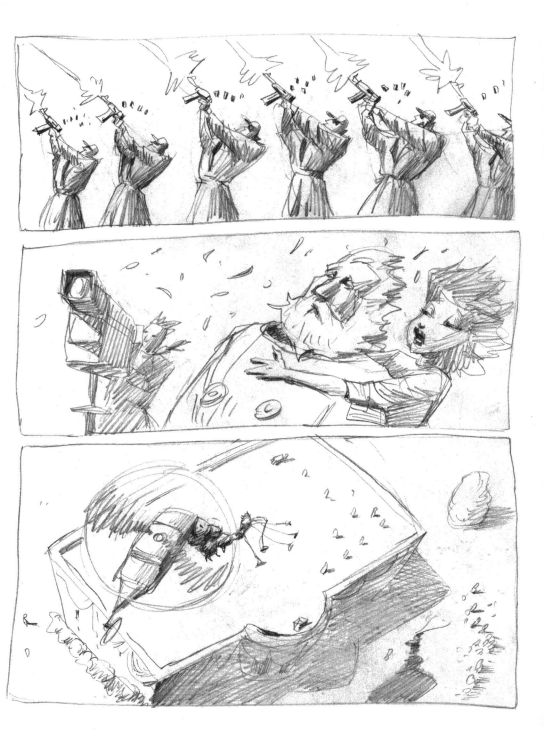

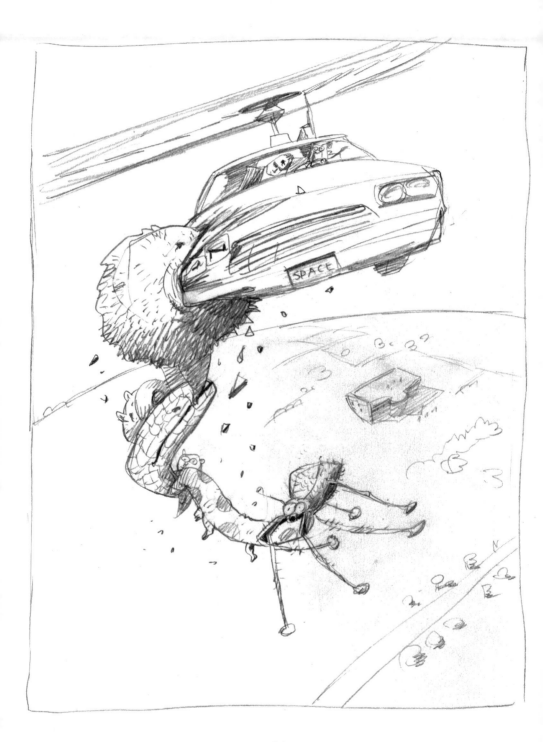

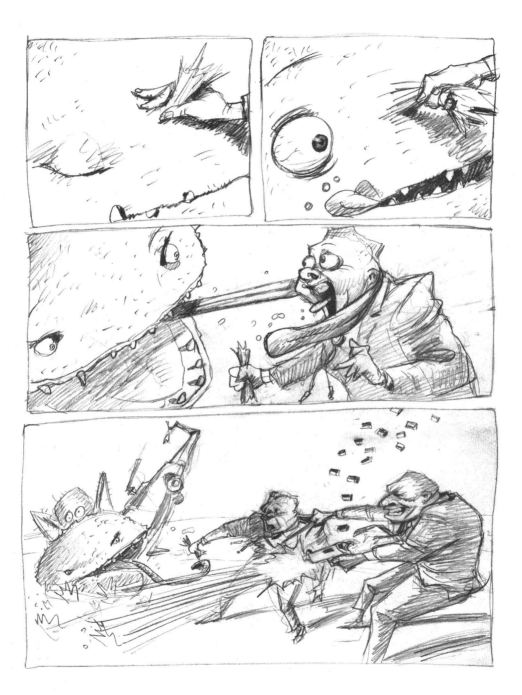

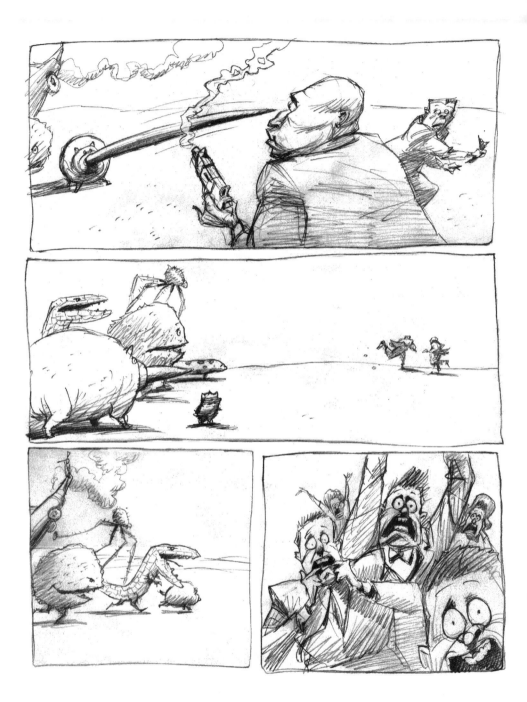

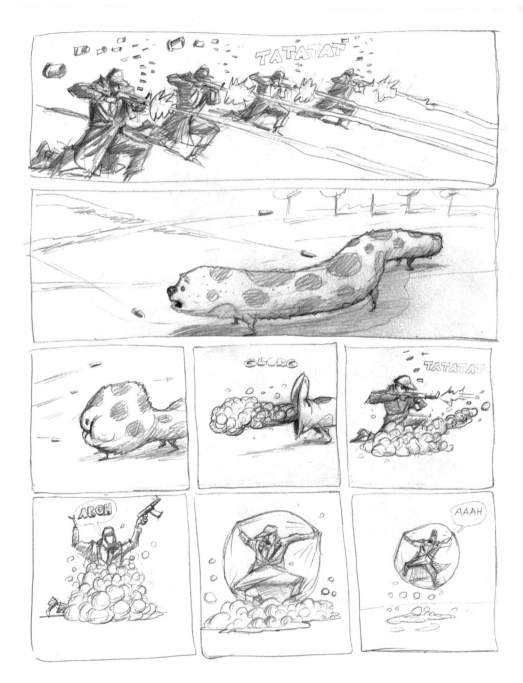

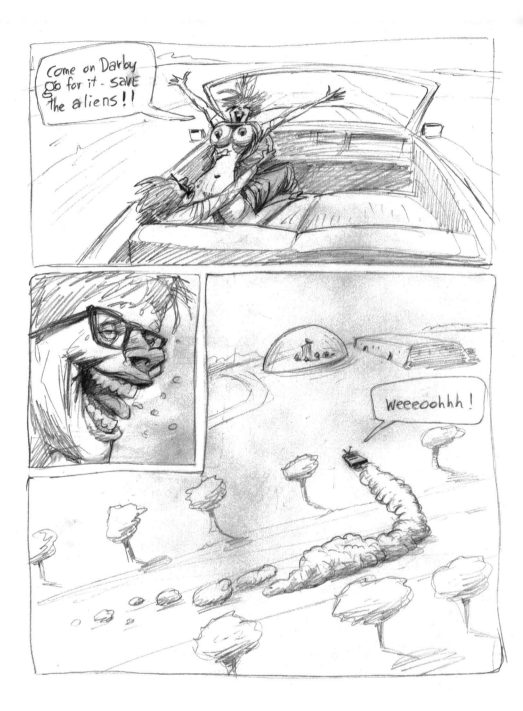

114

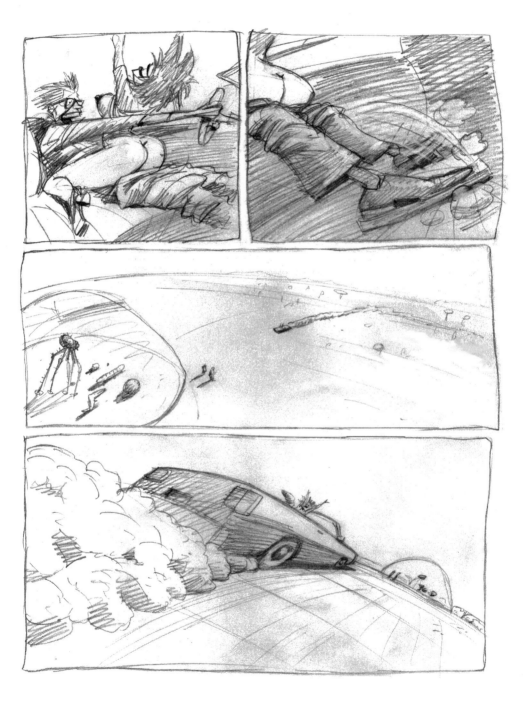

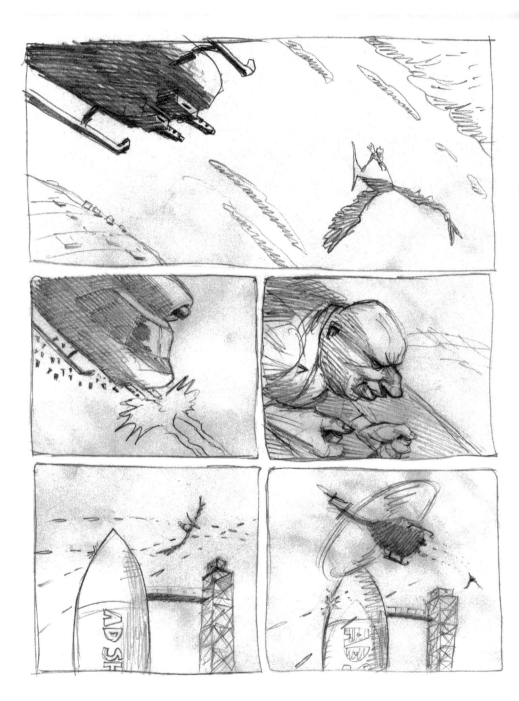

122

123

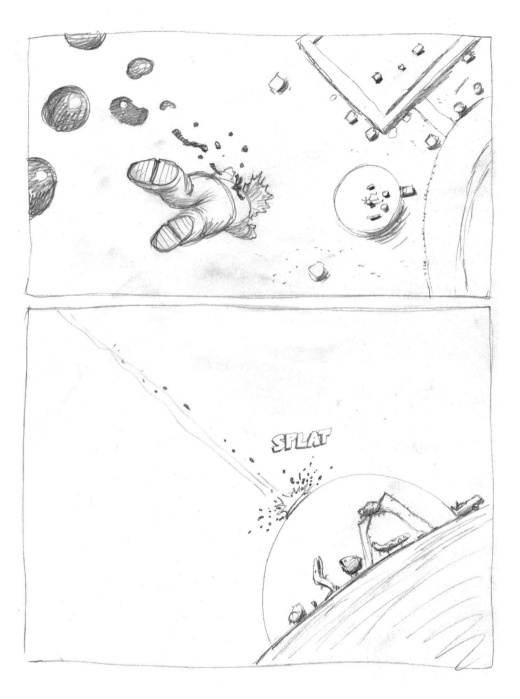

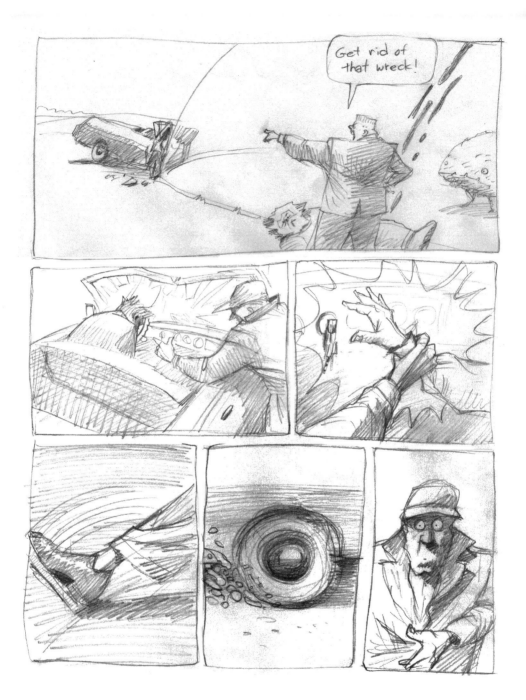

130

134

137

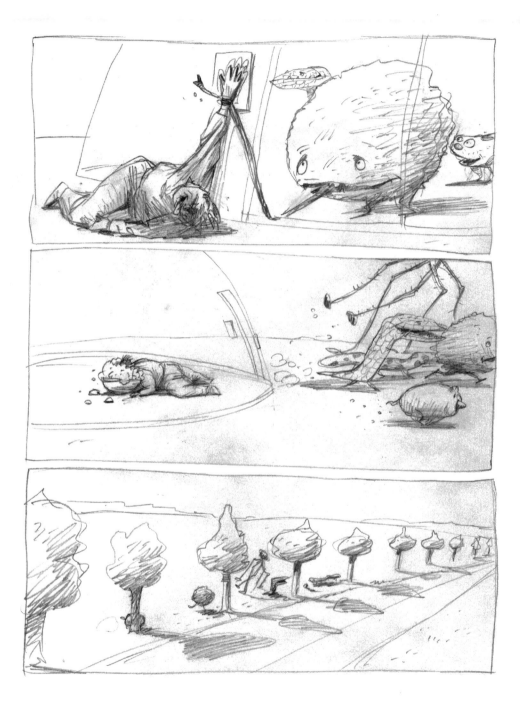

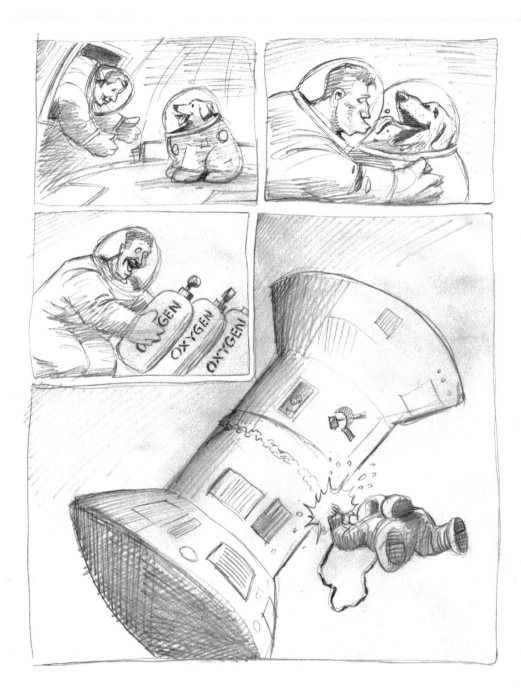

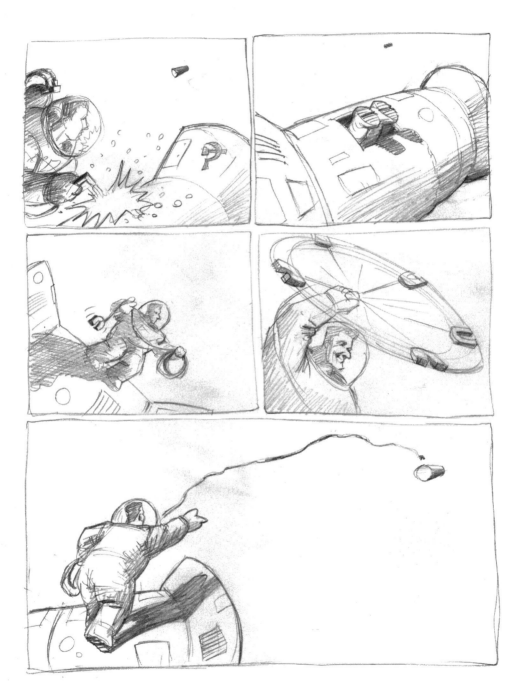

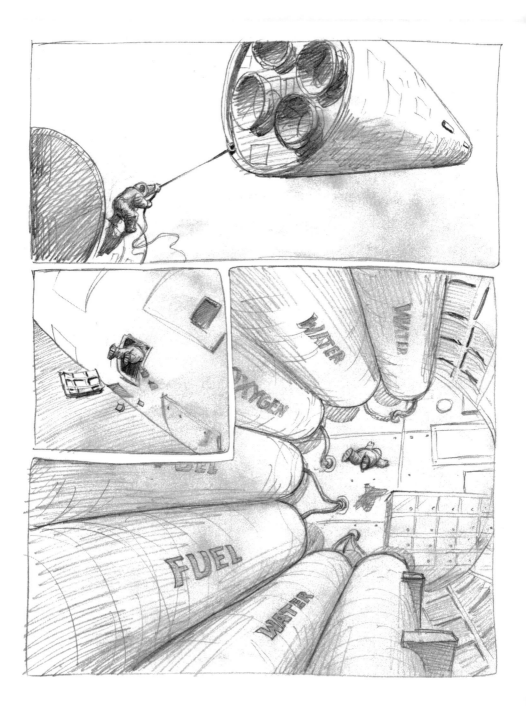

144

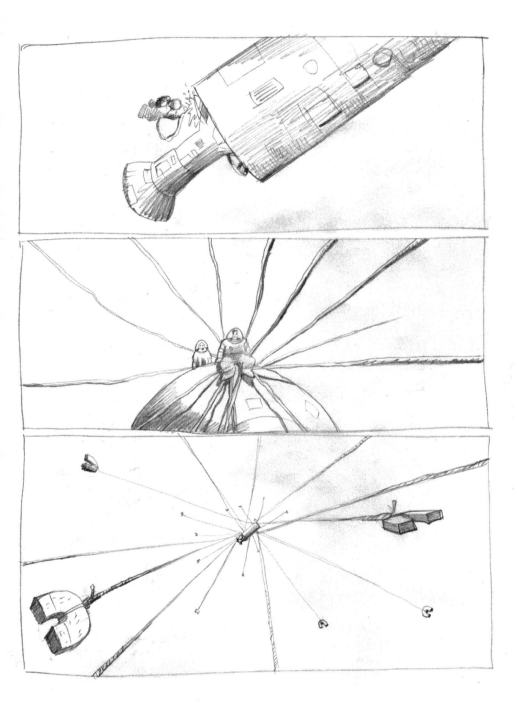

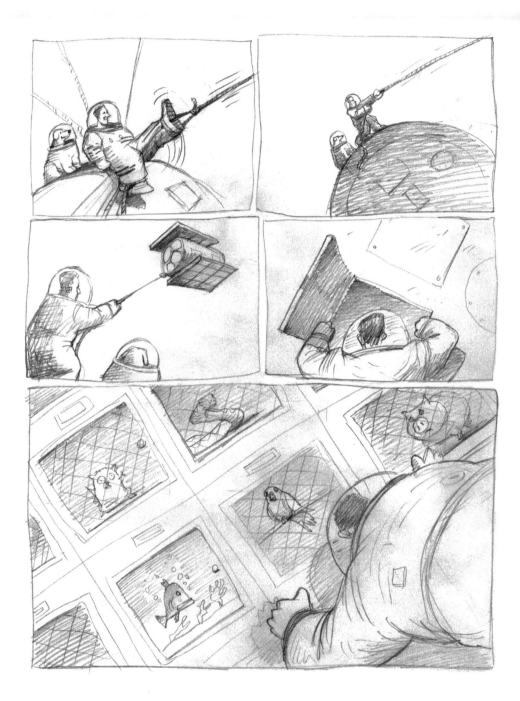

146

months later

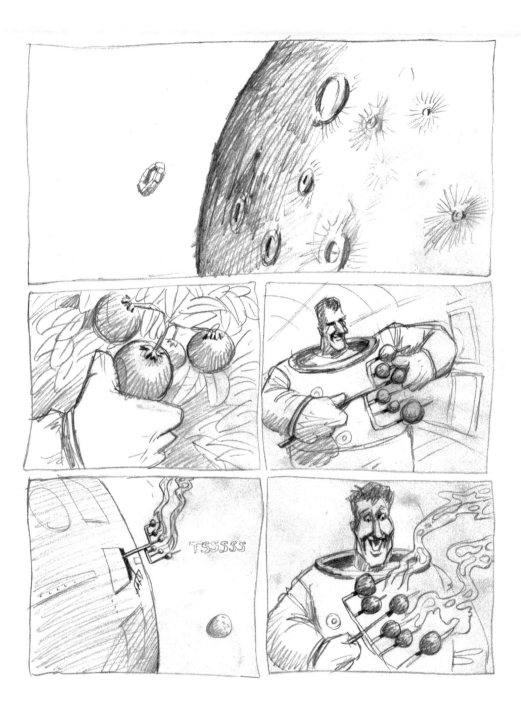

150

151

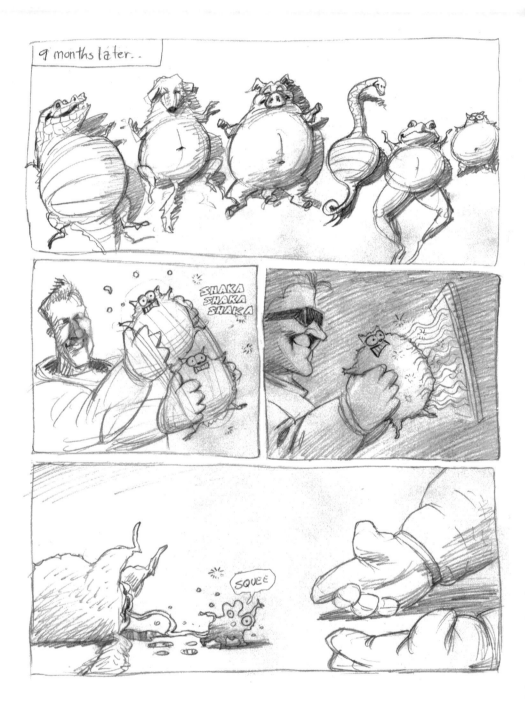

154

157

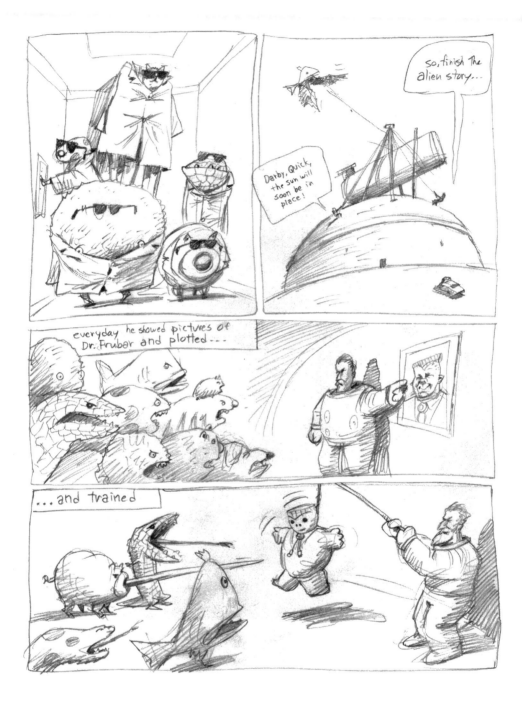

158

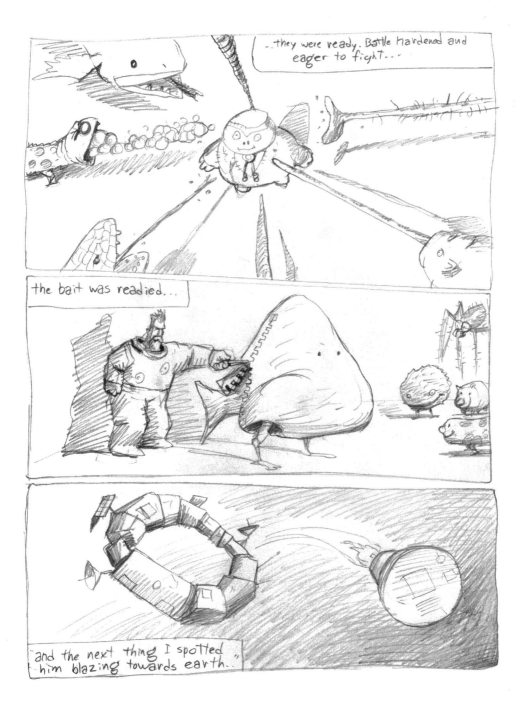

160

162

165

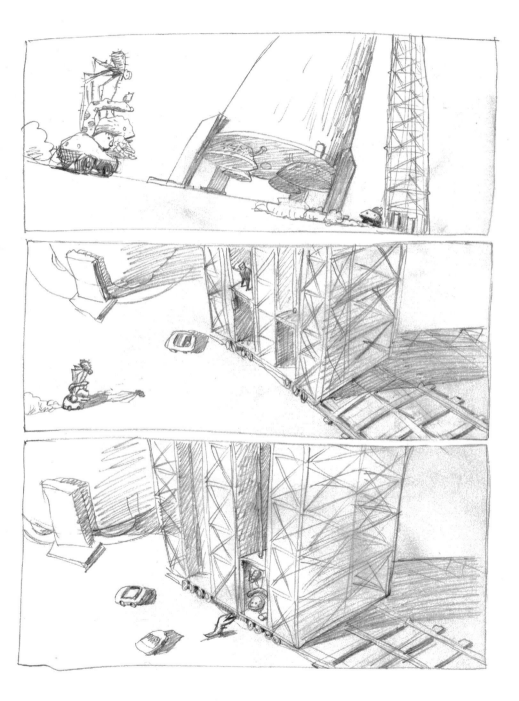

167

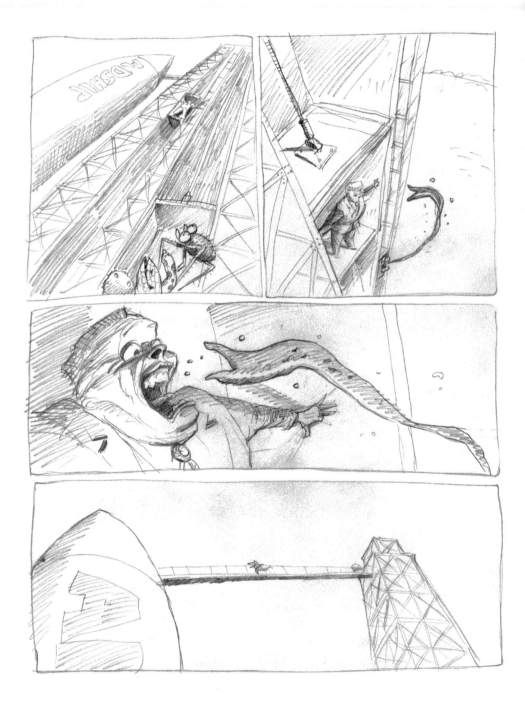

169

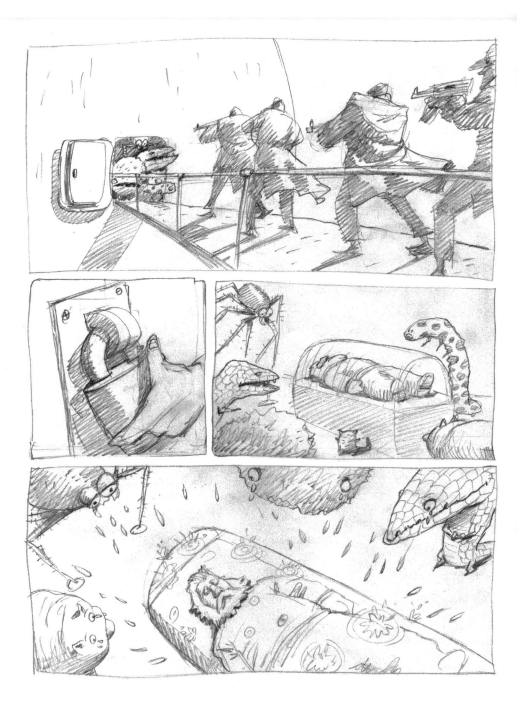

171

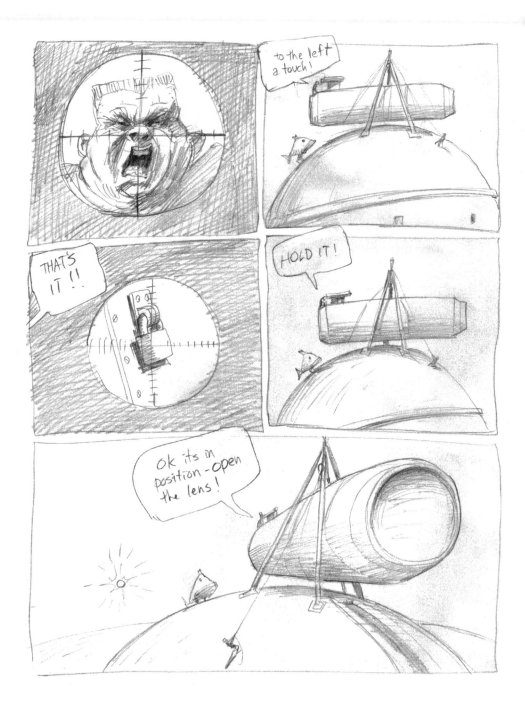

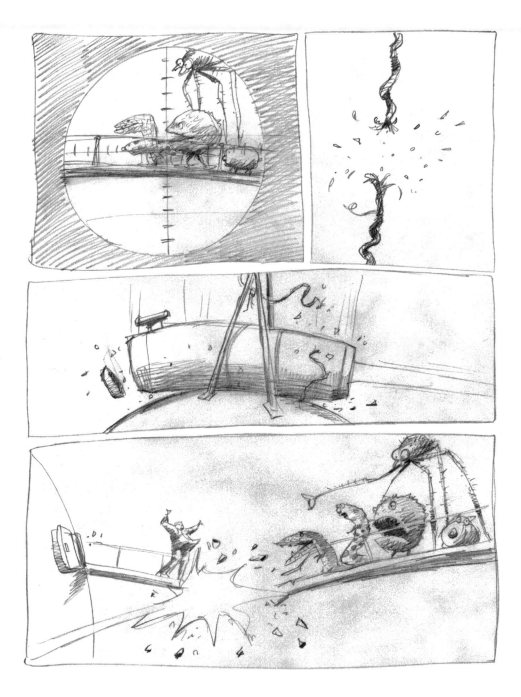

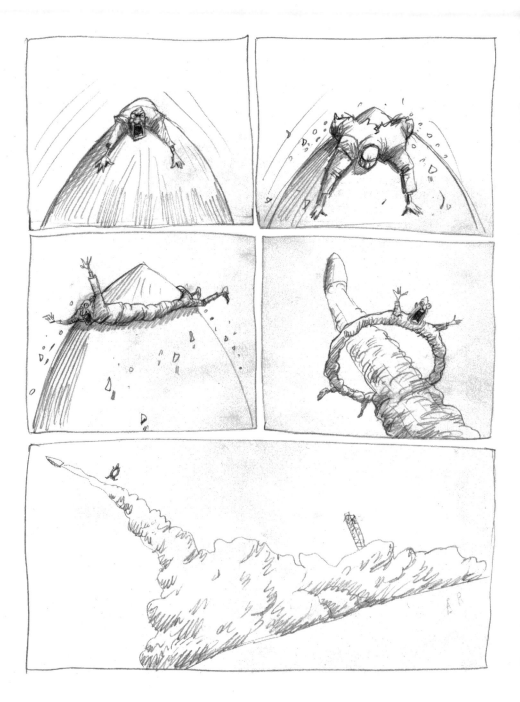

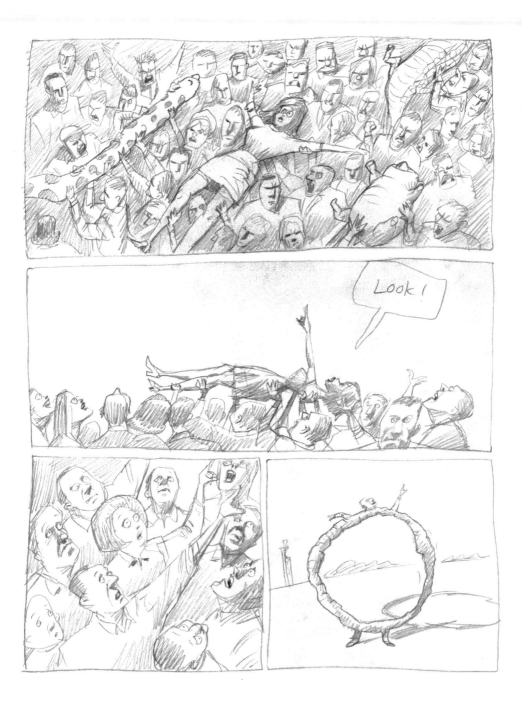

Later...

Alien
Petting
Zoo

Also available:
Confessions of a Cereal Eater, $17.95
Silent Invasion:
   vols. 1-2, $16.95
   vol. 3, $9.95
   vol. 4, $9.95

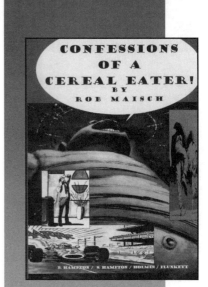

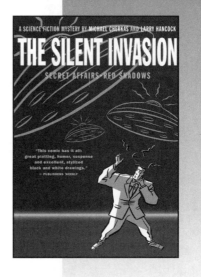

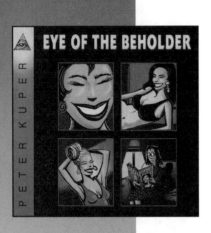